Aunt Carmen's
Book *of* Practical Saints

PAT MORA

Aunt Carmen's
Book *of* Practical Saints

BEACON PRESS

BOSTON

Beacon Press
25 Beacon Street
Boston, Massachusetts 02108-2892

Beacon Press books
are published under the auspices of
the Unitarian Universalist Association of Congregations.

Translation of the carol in "The Nativity / El Nacimiento": Vamos
todos a Belén / Con amor y gozo / Adoremos al Señor / Nuestro
Redentor. Let us go to Bethlehem / Joyfully and full of love / We'll
adore our Sacred Lord / Our Redeemer.

Translation of the lullaby in "Saint Anne / Santa Ana": Rru-rru-que-
rru-rru, que tan, tan, tan, Señora Santa Ana, carita de luna, Duerme
esta niña, que tengo en la cuna. Lady Saint Anne, little moon-face,
please lull this child in the crib to sleep.

02 01 00 99 98 97 8 7 6 5 4 3 2 1

Book design and typesetting by Lucinda Hitchcock

LIBRARY OF CONGRESS CATALOGING-IN-PUBLICATION DATA
Mora, Pat.
    Aunt Carmen's book of practical saints / Pat Mora.
        p.   cm.
    ISBN 0-8070-7206-0
        1. Christian poetry, American.   2. Saints – Poetry   I. Title.
    PS3563.073A9   1997   97-14422
    811'.54 – dc21

For the faith –
of my editor, Deborah Chasman,
my friend, Murray Bodo, and my early
heroines, the Sisters of Loretto

Contents

Aunt Carmen's
Book *of* Practical Saints

Prayer to the Saints |

Oración a los Santos

At sixteen I began to pray to you, old friends,
    for a handsome man who would never stray.
        Devoutly, I'd say,
Saint Peter the Apostle,
    please grant me this miracle,
Saint Raphael, the Archangel,
    remove every obstacle,
San José, dear father,
    may he frown at liquor
Saint Clare,
        for Mother, could he be a millionaire,
Saint John Nepomuk,
    my few faults may he overlook,
Santa María Magdalena,
    que a veces me sirva mi cena,
Saint Christopher,
    may he my figure prefer,
Our Lady of Remedies,
        could he avoid my father's frugalities,
Saint Francis,
        please don't make him a pessimist,
Saint Anne,
    could he be a very handsome man,
Saint Anthony,
    may he know the art of flattery,
Santa Bárbara, protector against lightning,
    make him good at dancing,
Saint Genevieve,
    may he never plot to deceive,
Saint Blaise,
    let him shower me with praise,
Saint Jerome,
    have him build me my dream-home,

San Pascual,
>   como él que no haya igual,
Saint Patrick,
>   could he be a lovesick Catholic,
Saint Gertrude the Great,
>   forgive me, but make him passionate,
Saint Lucy,
>   suggest he kiss me secretly,
Saint Martin,
>   may my smile turn him to gelatin,
Santa Teresita,
>   que me traiga florecitas,
Saint Agnes,
>   make him love me with wild excess,
Saint James,
>   por favor, nudge him this love to proclaim,
Saint Rose,
>   have him soon propose,
Saint Elizabeth,
>   may we celebrate our fiftieth,
Saint Jude,
>   let me soon be wooed,
Saint Stephen,
>   please remind all the santos
>   to find me a husband soon. Ah, men. Amen.

Saint Martin of Porres |
San Martín de Porres

Can I sing you, Brother Martin,
saint whose hands know work, like mine?
Would that we could sit together,
tell our cuentos, sip some wine.

Soon I'll close the church till morning.
Please guide me walking home alone.
Not a safe place for a woman.
Justice this old world postpones.

Speaking to our sweeping rhythms,
let us plot for those in need.
Can't you scare these stubborn faithful,
with your powers intercede?

Bread you gave to those in hunger,
kindness to the child alone,
held the trembling hand that suffered,
kindness from a man disowned.

Is it true when you were sweeping,
cats and dogs would come to chat,
telepathically you'd answer,
query disbelieving rats?

Brother Broom, with just a handshake,
you could cure a soul in pain.
Oh, I wish that you could touch me,
make these old joints fresh again.

Would that you had time to teach me
bilocation, such a trick,
not that I deserve the honor
and pleading seems impolitic.

You liked flying and liked gardens,
so practice aerial delights.
Come see rosas, tulips, daisies.
Can't I whet your appetite?

Ay, that I had seen the shining,
from your oratorio,
in your habit, man so prayerful,
that your very self would glow.

How we come, the dark-skinned faithful,
comforted to see you here,
able to confide our sorrows
to a black man's willing ear.

Your corrido I must finish
for priests frown at such casual songs,
frowning is their special talent,
but still, protect them all night long.

Help me listen to my garden,
cease wrinkled judgments based on skin,
our colored sacks like bulbs or seeds
that hold our fragrant selves within.

Saint Gertrude the Great |

Santa Gertrudis la Magna

One day you appeared,
una niña amid their stern, black habits
that wagged fingers at your little voice.
At first maybe you even whined
when at five they expected you to study,
memorize your lessons and prayers by heart.

Surely, alone you wondered in your heart
if your parents would one day appear.
When the nuns prayed or ate, you'd study
their unrevealing faces and habits,
notice who let you sip her wine,
daydreamed which might be your mother's voice.

In time, you heard a voice,
a calling deep in your heart,
a longing, prayers for years intertwined
and after careful preparation, you appeared
in your first uncomfortable yet welcome habit.
Your sisters hugged, and you continued your study.

Since every day was a Sunday
in the cloister, you learned your silent voice,
releasing it in prayer became a habit.
You'd stare at Christ's heart
for hours until all else disappeared,
your rapture like wine.

He whispered, "Divine delights like wine."
How did you feel when Christ spoke? You studied
His eyes on you, His face and lips which appeared
to be smiling. His voice
filled you, and you stared at His heart,
unaware now of even your rough habit.

Grateful for your devotional habit
and having promised celestial wine,
Christ motioned, and you leaned on His Sacred Heart,
heard it, beating. You studied
its holy rhythm, dizzy in His voice.
Christ and Mary appeared and reappeared.

I study you and this writing about rapture like wine.
Christ appeared, and you heard His fragrant voice.
Ay, Gran Santa, teach us this habit of releasing our
hearts.

Saint Barbara |

Santa Bárbara

Forgive the knife, dear Santita.
　　Again I must protect my casita
　　　　with a sliver from your statue.

Hear the lightning? At home, I'll just throw
　　this bit of you in the fire, its glow
　　　　and a quick prayer. We'll be safe.

What did you see high in your tower?
　　Did your father's eyes really devour
　　　　you like an apple tart?

He locked you up so none but he
　　could touch your hair or ever see
　　　　the smile you saved.

　　　　　　　　¡Qué padre tan bárbaro!

The silence led you to wonder
　　if humans can discover
　　　　why we're born.

Then from your tower you overheard
　　a Christian voice. It seemed absurd
　　　　to live without such faith.

Wishing to make your faith concrete,
　　you asked for a third window, complete
　　　　symbol of the Trinity.

Pagan but no fool, your father
　　raged, ordered your torture.
　　　　But you would not repent.

　　　　　　　　¡Qué padre tan bárbaro!

¡Ay! Men's power to cause us pain
    if we begin to ascertain
        that we can think. ¡Dios mío!

He lost control and grabbed your hair,
    picked up an ax, hacked your bare
        neck and lightning struck.

A sizzling end. Today a movie
    would be made. Talk hosts in ecstasy
        would grill the architect.

The pieces of the bloody story
    are familiar as jujubes
        I've savored in movies' dark.

Why are we taught to like the taste
    of blood and suffering, a waste
        to salivate at evil.

Santita, help me daily to create
    a prayerful solitude, to wait
        for quiet, inner light.

Our Lady of Guadalupe |
Nuestra Señora de Guadalupe

In her bed, she waited for light. Her voice rising
with the sun, wandered through our dark house
like a thin river, gathered our sleepy
melodies, braiding us together.

Cantemos el alba.
Ya viene el día.

What would my children say if from
my blue wool blanket, I sang at dawn,
like my grandmother, let my old voice lift
me, release my body to playful prayer?

Let us sing ma-tins.

Today knees as promised will polish
this aisle, as mine have, shuffled to thank you
for my first perfect grandbaby, each
finger, toe, her eyes glowing like candles.

Day-light is com-ing.

That morning, like my abuela, I danced
in your honor, Brown Mother, in my room
alone, said to my feet, "No shyness. Dance
to the rhythm of our baby's breath."

Cantemos el alba.

My bare feet lifted from the wood I've swept
for years, such joy carried me into
music birds know, freedom to fly, willful
ignorance of theories like gravity.

Ya viene el día.

Perhaps I imagined the four of us
drifting out the window, dancing over
the desert, Our Lady's stars swirling
in praise over prisms glinting in snow.

Let us sing ma-tins.
Day-light is com-ing.

I kneel to gather my distracted self,
eyes closed. Ay, Virgencita y Abuelita,
all heavenly mothers, help me live faith,
a woman whose prayers dance and sing.

The Nativity |

El Nacimiento

Va-mos to-dos a Be-lén,
Con a-mor y go-zo,
A-dor-e-mos al Se-ñor,
Nues-tro Re-den-tor.

Va-mos to-dos a Be-lén,
Old friends take your places,
Move us with your stance of awe,
Snare us with your gaze.

Con a-mor y go-zo,
You, sweet Jesus, I must hide,
Wrap in this soft blanket,
Croon you lullabies.

A-dor-e-mos al Se-ñor,
Weeks I've been preparing,
Making of my heart a place,
Love can spring again.

Nues-tro Re-den-tor.
Stars I'll bring down for these trees,
For light we long to enter,
Faith our fears release.

Va-mos to-dos a Be-lén,
Through snow, we gather seeking
Peace on earth, ourselves transformed,
May hope be born again.

The Holy Child of Atocha |
El Santo Niño de Atocha

My neighbor says she's very sorry
To have locked you in a chest.
Keep her son where she can see him,
And she won't feel so hard-pressed.

Nachita wishes she could come.
As thanks she sends these tiny shoes.
Tonight please wear what she crocheted
On your evening rendezvous.

> Agua y pan, agua y pan,
> Agua y pan, your nighttime song.

You hear about her gnarled knees.
When young, like you these hills we knew,
If Mother caught us out at night,
We wished we were in Timbuktu.

Mothers worry now like then,
How I did scold my children too,
Shook their trembling shoulders
If they dared be overdue.

> Agua y pan, agua y pan,
> Agua y pan, your nighttime song.

Of all your travels, let me sing,
Sweet Holy Child out alone,
Descending into mines or wells,
Quick to hear a prisoner's groan.

Long ago, you smiled at Moors,
Then entered prison moans in Spain.
You've soothed our pueblo's men at war,
Led wounded uncles home again.

Agua y pan, agua y pan,
Agua y pan, your nighttime song.

In the company of cats,
Daring darkness, off you wander,
Down our lonely streets, you trudge
Small, intrepid rescuer.

"Mis gatitos, buenos amigos,
"Come. Agua y pan for friends in need."
Your meowing congregation gathers,
Follows you at slinking speed.

Agua y pan, agua y pan,
Agua y pan, your nighttime song.

Moon sends down her sky-wide smile,
At tails raised high for night's journey,
You and your whiskered retinue,
March off with audacity.

Your mother worries, but she knows
This earth needs what you bring to us,
With gourd and basket ever full,
Your nourishment's miraculous.

Agua y pan, agua y pan,
Agua y pan, your nighttime song.

At dawn, you and your cats return.
They flee, and you trudge down this aisle,
Your shoes again a holey mess.
Till I arrive, you doze awhile.

Through the years, you're always young,
While mirrors now can frighten me.
But I'll keep hobbling while I can.
Like our old dog, stubbornly.

> Agua y pan, agua y pan,
> Agua y pan, your nighttime song.

We love your size, a formal boy,
Chiquito, help us follow you,
Pilgrims who each bring our gifts,
Pursuing good, wear out our shoes.

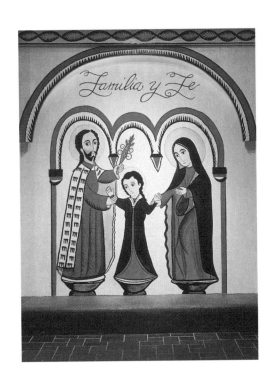

The Holy Family |
    La Sagrada Familia

We are like butterflies,
Safe between their hands,
Safe between their hands,
Sweet Jesus, do you also remember
Your parents' echoed reprimands,
Their echoed reprimands?

You know I snitched candies.
Scoldings, and sent to pray,
Scolded and sent to pray.
I'd bang the table,
Preview of judgment day,
That scary judgment day.

Stubborn, I often whined,
Sought singularity,
My singularity,
But we know parents hover,
Even in dreams, they worry.
Even in dreams, worry.

When I tried lipstick,
I was, they said, too young,
Always, I was too young.
I erred and started yelling,
Lashing from mother tongue,
Lashing, my mother's tongue.

And men – they found none good enough,
But nunhood not for me.
No. Nunhood not for me.
So I married the sober teacher,
A man with a pedigree.
Like you, Saint Joseph, a good pedigree.

Now I've raised children,
Held them between my hands,
Such promise between these hands,
My hair is grayer.
Mary, you understand,
I know you understand.

Eighty, I'm still their child,
Safer between their hands,
Even now, safety's between their hands,
Up there, I hear them hover,
Raining down their old commands,
On my gray, still raining their commands.

We are like butterflies,
Protected in our homes,
Blessed, if protected in our homes.
Help us savor the sweetness
Of family honeycombs,
Our family honeycombs.

Saint Joseph |

San José

I wonder if fathers above congregate,
sip and brag about their clever children.
If so, you are in charge. I speculate
you daydream about your earthly years when
you'd surprise your son with what your hands made
while he played with some stray dog or cat.
You'd concoct some hide-and-seek charade,
like Papá hand Him the toy with the caveat
that He run and show His mother who'd smile
and rock the wood bird or lamb in her palm.
Your hands sheltered wife and son, fulfilled
our human duty as sung in the psalms.

San José, teach fathers your gentle way,
how playfulness, like prayer, sweetens the day.

Our Lady of the Annunciation |
Nuestra Señora de la Anunciación

"Rejoice!" the angel Gabriel said.

And it came to pass, a young maiden
blessed among women, found grace
within, bore a son named Emmanuel.

These painters all think you passive.
Do they fear your fire, María?
This old world still scared of women.
Were you praying inside when you heard
the feathered words? I see you lulled
by the afternoon breeze and light,
waiting for José, stitching your hope
into a small blanket, the rhythm
of your hand unconscious as breathing.

Light enters you through every pore,
dissolves you into itself.
Fearless, you look straight into
the blinding sun and burn in love.
From within or above, such borders
blurred, you hear, "Rejoice!" Ablaze,
you rise changed into the world,
wrap your arms around your shine,
helping your skin to hold such joy.

As if from far, far away, you hear
your neighbor's afternoon singing
"The fig tree putteth forth her green . . ."
a lavender breeze carrying you
inside. Full knowing, your spirit
expands as you stir herb soup
from your garden. Even the spoon glows.
With every breath, you praise God,
and your smile refuses to hide.

"Rejoice!" the voice said.

And it came to pass, a young maiden
blessed among women, found grace
within, bore a son, Emmanuel.

As Goodness grew in you, Mother,
may the Holy Spirit glow in us.

The Stations of the Cross |
La Vía Crucis

Again I'll walk with you, Dear Lord. Forgive me.
These knees won't bend. I can't genuflect.

> ¡Ay, qué tristeza!

I fear your Carmen failed this week. Why don't I walk
with those who need me? I live tangled in myself.

> ¡Ay, qué tristeza!

Pilate washed his hands of judging you. I judge,
bang my silent gavel at those who enter here.

> ¡Ay, qué tristeza!
> ¡Ay, qué dolor!

Since last Friday, how many came to me carrying crosses
that I didn't see, tangled in myself?

> ¡Ay, qué tristeza!
> ¡Ay, qué dolor!

I would have reached out when you fell, I think, but I
didn't risk frowns, reach out to Juan who carries AIDS.

> ¡Ay, qué tristeza!
> ¡Ay, qué dolor!

You comfort your mother, all mothers. Why don't I
comfort Ana whose daughter carries a fatherless baby?

> ¡Ay, qué tristeza!
> ¡Ay, qué dolor!

Weekly I walk this sad path with you, sigh at blood
and thorns, but unlike Simon I resist, tangled in myself.

> ¡Ay, qué tristeza
> > ¡Ay, qué dolor!

Veronica wipes your face with her veil, risks herself.
I stay swaddled safe in my pieties.

> ¡Ay, qué tristeza!
> > ¡Ay, qué dolor!

You fall again, weak from the weight of cruelties. I
wrinkle my nose at those who come in old clothes.

> ¡Ay, qué tristeza!
> > ¡Ay, qué dolor!

The women come toward you. Would I
have muttered at the stumbling spectacle of you?

> ¡Ay, qué tristeza!
> > ¡Ay, qué dolor!

At your last fall, you clutch the earth.
Passive, I watch my hands folded, useless.

> ¡Ay, qué tristeza!
> > ¡Ay, qué dolor!

Stripped, gagging on gall, you look at me,
your smug Carmen and her wagging finger.

> ¡Ay, qué tristeza!
> > ¡Ay, qué dolor!

I hear hammering, nails into your flesh. I hammer,
YOU SHOULD, YOU SHOULD at everyone, my hurtful litany.

¡Ay, qué tristeza!
¡Ay, qué dolor!

Your spirit leaves your body as mine will soon.
Our pueblo will be rid of my stiff righteousness.

¡Ay, qué tristeza!

Taken down from the Cross your body is cold. Forgive
your Carmen's icy heart. Why don't my meditations alter me?

¡Ay, qué tristeza!

In your tomb, your bruised body waits. Help me
to forget my old self, to let my light shine through.

Death |

La Muerte

You don't belong, fea Doña Sebastiana.

Some pull you in a rock-filled cart,
a penance they impose
when the priest's not looking.
They fear his frowns.
He fears mine and well he should.

I've cleaned this church
for over forty years, swept,
mopped, dusted, sewed for my saints,
kept them company, my chatter
like butterflies around
the flowers and candles I refresh.
"Shhhh. It's not your house,"
my husband whispers, as if I don't know
it's the holy home of mi Diosito,
home of Divine Order.
¡Ay! What must He think,
this modern religion with no backbone,
no Latin, no chanting, no confession,
no fiery scoldings, just priests frowning
and electric candles. A church that fears
fire – and women. The same world inside
and out. No transformation. No mystery.

Instead of organ music and a hidden
choir, voices drifting down,
soft as white feathers,
some churches are a circus, tambourines
and snare drums. Next they'll want
clowns to make the children laugh.
If they want entertainment,
tell them to stay home

or at the malls, their other homes.
Over my dead body, tambourines
and snare drums. They tried,
remember? I grabbed this broom
and swept them out the door,
smacked their ankles hard as I could.

The priest is scared
of me, and that's how I want it.
I've earned my space.
I know about scaring men.
Haven't I been married for sixty years?
Marriage works best
when men think we're volcanoes,
¿verdad, Comadre? Los hombres
walk more carefully around us then.

Over my dead body.

You don't scare me, Doña Sebastiana.
I see people walk around you,
their mouth open like yours.
May your unblinking eyes remind them
of the horror: an unholy death.
Let me bless myself to scare away
the thought. Not like my parents' death.
Their glowing souls slipped right into
the waiting hands of Jesus, Mary, and Joseph,
their two souls, fighters, yes, but moral.
When I use the word, my children
and grandchildren frown.
Truth makes them squirm
which shows their goodness.

Ash Wednesday. "Thou art dust
and unto dust though shalt return,"
the priest said today. He frowns
when I drag you from this closet at Lent.
You don't belong,

but I save what can be useful.
You're not official, yet you're persistent,
¿verdad, Comadre? You and I
can be informal. Dos viejitas.
You don't scare me.
I'll look you eye to eye.

Shoot, Doña Sebastiana. Go ahead.
Slipping out of this crumpled body
will probably feel good, like slipping off
my winter coat in spring. I'll feel
lighter, more my true self,
ready to visit with mis santos,
have a real conversation, revel
in their words, shining, like candles.

Christim on the Cross |

Nuestro Señor Crucificado

I couldn't sleep so came
to keep you company.
Dust will moan, gust,
seethe against the sun.
Today earth remembers.

Storms will howl their litany, whirlwind of memories drones.
Earth remembers, groans at your suffering. I couldn't sleep
and came to keep you company. Earth remembers the lash
tearing flesh, thorns piercing your brow and bone. Your
mother, alone, watches in shadows, nightmare of blood
streaming into the mouth she fed. I look up to your body on a
cross, the cross of your body. You cry thirsty for my
transformation, eighty years and still you look down at your
Carmen, selfish and proud. I want to wash away the streams
of blood. I seek the comfort of denial, but unknown blood still
streams. Here, mothers still watch alone. Morning of mourning.
Through dust we come, hear your last words, drum, flute,
music remembering our darkness, how we wound innocence and
cruelty condone, fold our hands protectively into ourselves.

I came to keep you company.
Dear Christ, who feels
the world's agony, help me
to open my stubborn arms,
fold into me those in need.

Saint Isidore the Farmer |
   San Ysidro Labrador

May our work enrich the earth. Hear our request.
A worker like us, but all day the Lord you'd address.
This night and at our death, in peace may we rest.

Early to the fields, but soon you'd lose interest,
Angels to your aid, reward for daily prayerfulness.
May our work enrich the earth. Hear our request.

We'll carry you in procession, our faith attest,
Sing and pray this evening that our fields you'll bless.
This night and at our death, en paz may we rest.

You see the dry land needs rain. Quick, send a tempest.
Enjoy your canopy but hear the need we express.
May our work enrich the earth. Hear our request.

Good life is rhythms as we poor workers know best.
To wake to this gold land, now that's true wealthiness.
This night and at our death, in peace may we rest.

Corn and trees glow in the sunset, grace manifest.
Send one of those hard-working angels to my address.
May our work enrich the earth. Hear our request.
This night and at our death, en paz may we rest.

The Holy Spirit |

   El Espíritu Santo

The priest says, "The wind, like ours, whirled.
Alleluia, alleluia.
Stir in your hearts the fire of love."
The young priest says God is not male.

The priest wears red vestments, reads to us
about the room of twelve men. Like birds,
flames dart above the apostles' heads.
The professor says God is not male.

The men spoke in tongues, holy fire
dwelled in them. "Alleluia.
Stir in your hearts the fire of love."
My granddaughter says God is not male.

I've seen old pictures and statues,
the Trinity as three men.
Father and Son, the God I know.
The young priest says God is not male.

The gospel says, "The Spirit of truth
dwells with you and is in you."
The priest says, "Lift up your heart."
The professor says God is not male.

Each bird I watch sail this wide sky
reminds me of you, Holy Spirit.
You dwell in us. Alleluia.
My granddaughter says God is not male.

Diosito, I come, daughter to
father. It's sad, but my old mind
can't imagine a woman god.
The young priest says God is not male.

The priest says, "The wind, like ours, whirled."
If it's like ours, the wind sang
its wild song, entered women or
men, all who welcomed its power.

The wind changed them like wind changes
mountains, alleluia, alleluia,
like our sun bakes adobe and bakes us,
like love, a candle, lights us from within.

Holy Spirit, I entrust myself
to you who speak all languages,
who dwells in us all, the spark
of good and peace, the pure white flame.

Alleluia, alleluia.
Stir in our hearts the fire of love.

Saint Pascal Baylon |

San Pascual Bailón

San Pascual Pastorcito,
larón, larón, larito,
spring breezes have me singing.
Don't you laugh at my bumpy voice.

Now what was I telling
you yesterday in my kitchen?
What bread we made.
A good seasoning, our conversations.

Books say you were a shepherd
who liked the smell of words.
Did you really ask strangers
to decipher the books you carried?

San Pascual Pastorcito,
larón, larón, larito,
You sang to your sheep, hungry
to solve the mystery of letters.

I wish I'd been your teacher.
You could have read to me,
in the music of a shade tree, eh?
Our words braiding with the breeze.

Your heart, so much bigger than mine,
teaches me. True, your stomach is too,
but I try not to offend mis santos.
Cleverly, you get revenge.

San Pascual Pastorcito,
what if I'd been a cook
at the Franciscan monastery
you came to in your patched clothes?

Soon a barefoot porter, you'd say,
"I was born poor, and I'll stay poor."
You'd sneak into the kitchen
to feed hungry eyes at the door.

You'd then whistle innocently,
spy mounds of delicacies,
hide the empanadas and bizcochitos
in the habit of your hands.

San Pascual Pastorcito
larón, larón, larito,
your pupil Carmen who counts pennies
would have rapped your knuckles with her spoon.

A prayerful place, your kitchen.
Ollas mysteriously simmered,
and in the clouds of fragrant steam
you prayed, floating in your faith.

Meat, onions and chiles were somehow diced.
Not that you didn't work too, peel
garlic shiny as dreams, evenings
you and your gatito asleep by the fire.

San Pascual Pastorcito,
larón, larón, larito,
before the altar too, your goodness lifted you,
devotion stronger than gravity.

Like all saints, you're a mirror.
We make of you what we need.
Teach me the sweet taste of generosity,
and also your practical culinary trickery.

Saint Rita |
Santa Rita

Wind, rain, fog this morning,
Santita. The sky and I brood.
The bell tolls. I'll light us some candles.
The sight of them eases the chill.

Last night, I listened to the river's
lullaby, stubborn old winder.
What tears and sighs it carries,
sorrows whispered for generations.

My neighbor, Alma, sewed you a new dress
as she promised long ago. You and Alma
live happy in her casita, ¿no? Two women
who endured the thorn of cruel husbands.

I'd whisper to her when she'd come, bruised,
crying, covering her face
so my husband wouldn't see her red
shame. "Pray to Santa Rita. She understands."

Too scared at first even to confide
in you, a woman who knew shame,
your spirit and jaw punched, you who
folded yourself inside into a speck.

If only your parents had listened
to your call, but they'd waited so long
for you. Your mother cried to think
of her girl swallowed by a convent.

So instead you were swallowed whole
by your husband's hungry hands, like Alma.
My husband pounded on their door,
but what locks her monster had on his heart.

Did your neighbors also try? Ay,
the night I kicked Alma's door in the snow,
and ese hombre flung water on my
burning face and slammed the door.

Your husband ruined your two boys, I think.
Three corpses, bodies you'd bathed and loved
now cold, stiff as trees. You must have cried
rivers over there in Italy, inside a fog.

Then you could pound on the convent door,
unencumbered by your men, follow your call.
"Non e virgine!" slammed the door.
Ay, the old song, virgins and virtues.

I've said, "Look, Father, the body
is complicated. The mind, worse."
But, pobrecitos, how can priests understand?
Those who make rules seldom understand.

Like the river, you were stubborn,
and you kept knocking on that door,
three tries, like in all good stories.
Once inside, you fasted and prayed.

Hours you stared at Christ on the crucifix,
begged Him to let you suffer too –
as if you hadn't, your three bodies
stiff as winter trees.

Your longing for pain, like a magnet yanked
a thorn from Christ's crown, smack
into your forehead. ¡Ay! The wound,
in a sense self-inflicted, festered.

Its smell like a foul fog swirled
into every room you entered, the wound
your proof of virtue and love, your blood
erasing other blood.

All this makes me think I should start
cleaning. Like Saint Rose, yours is a story
of thorns, smells, blooms. The other nuns
covered their noses for fifteen years.

Roses bloomed out of season at your death.
Their pink scent lingers in the convent
and around the glass coffin
in which your exhausted body rests.

Now your statue has a new dress.
Alma enjoys spoiling you.
Help us to follow our heart's call and please
help me to find some calmer married saints.

Where are the santas, not virgins, martyrs, widows?
Women who sigh, of course. All women sigh, but
women who laugh, kiss, cook, pray, struggle
so from within, their holy spirit will shine.

The Visitation |
La Visitación

Our stomachs bumped
when we hugged. How
we laughed, my comadre
and I, expecting our first,
full of wonder at our bodies'
secret life. Like yours, ours
met in that dark, our hands feeling
mysterious stirrings. Your cousin
called you blessed, María, when,
at Gabriel's news, you quickly
climbed the hills to Judah, savored
the moment of holding your friend.
Years she'd whispered her gray
sadness. At the music of your
voice, Elizabeth and baby leapt.
Three months you shared joy,
sewed like my comadre and me,
fed one another peaches,
moved through the garden
and rooms swelling with
grace. Dear Mother, help
me daily to give birth
to joy, to sharing
this life.

Saint Anthony of Padua |

San Antonio de Padua

Por favor, a little nod this morning?
Gracias. Now I know you forgive
your Carmen her wicked ways.
Like yours, may my tongue burn with faith.

Did they pour petitions in your ears
this weekend? "Por favor, San Antonio,
find my key, wallet, ring, husband."
Like yours, may their tongues burn with faith.

No church big enough for the crowds
that pressed toward the fire in your words,
¿verdad? You preached in markets, fields.
Like yours, then the faithful tongues burned.

Even bees, sparrows, fish quivered
at your words, lifted little faces
to the fire of your music,
like yours, their tongues burning in praise.

Forgive me while I dust your head,
so bald, mi San Antonio, remember
when I screamed, "Pelón, find my girls
or else." May I not burn for my words.

And when the voice said, "We found
your son," how I ran to the well, pulled
your head out, wrapped you in a towel,
crooned, "Ya, ya," my tongue burning in thanks.

All day I carried you in my arms
like I carried my babies, kissing
your little bald head, mi peloncito
querido who sets my tongue on fire.

I know you hated being upside down
for two weeks, but whose fault was it?
Ya, ya. He survived the war – you, the well.
Like yours, may his tongue burn with faith.

Mira, Santito, a fresh candle,
from your Carmen's heart heavy
with regret, a flame like your tongue
burning bright when your body dried to dust.

Here, let me dust El Santo Niño
who floated down to your burning
words, wrapped His chubby arms around
your neck, smiled at your holy fire.

Yes, I promise. I only hide Him when
you're stubborn, like the time you wouldn't find
the money I'd hidden from my husband.
Like yours, how my tongue burned with faith.

Though it hurts, I'll kneel. No threats,
talk of wells, but please even after sixty years,
help me find the patience to remain married.
A little nod? Good, may I burn with faith.

Querido San Antonio, hear us
who bring our dark doubts and fears.
Help us find the Holy Spirit within.
Like yours, may our tongues burn with faith.

Saint Liberata |
Santa Librada

I hide you in a drawer. "No female bodies,"
the priest frowns. "Don't bring those crazy legends
into this church. No women on crosses."
I read, old book in old hands, the mystery,
the history of pain, but men don't listen.
I share your story with other women.

I tell them of your mother, a woman
with nine baby girls growing in her body
while the king salivates for sons. She just listens.
Why do we seem so passive in legends,
pretty ornaments? It's a mystery
since the women I know, know crosses.

Your father raged, far more than cross
at a castle full of worthless women.
He schemed as you called him "Daddy," a mystery
that anyone could plot to hurt such bodies.
While I sweep, I'd best hide my book of legends.
Here comes the priest, and I don't want to listen.

When you heard of Christ's suffering, you listened.
In love, you pledged yourself to His Cross,
joy in giving yourself, like the legendary
saints, but your father plotted, since women
could be good for trade, their soft bodies
negotiable, the ownership mystery.

You refused to marry, the mystery
of your faith and bravery as you listened
to your papa's leers, rantings, shaking your body.
You prayed for ugliness before your Cross,
longed to scare away the sweaty palms, a woman
just wanting to own her body is the legend.

Hair flowed – a beard and mustache, says the legend.
Your papa crucified you, the mystery
of men who wound children and women.
You spoke of burdens, and those who listened
heard your whispered promise from your cross
to ease the sadness of suffering bodies.

Holy Spirit, all bodies are crosses
and joys. Help me listen to the legends
of women who honor their mystery.

Saint Mary Magdalen |
Santa María Magdalena

"Her sins, which are many, are forgiven,"
Christ said, looking down at the dark rivers
of your hair, your head bowed, repentant.

For years, I thought of you as the great Sinner
with a capital S, a woman of the flesh
who made my tías frown, a paramour.

I stared at your image, at Christ's bare feet enmeshed
in the swirls of your hair. You kneel, bow low,
bathe His feet with your tears, such sorrowfulness.

You rub the tangle of your hair although
polite society frowns that you dare dry
His feet with yourself, a beautiful tableau.

Opening your alabaster box, you apply
perfumes, sweet essences. You defy
sour mutters, kiss His feet, the righteous horrify.

Soft, your hands stroke Christ openly, not shy.
You are not tangled in the myth that flesh is evil
until men write your story. They simplify.

They say you flee to the desert, with a skull
and Cross, a wanton woman alone
in a cave, her banishment self-willed.

For years, I too thought you should atone
for smoldering, but who are we to judge you,
prim critics in our pompous monotone?

The body foul and wicked? Untrue.
We count your seven devils when we
have a dozen each. My sins aren't few.

"Thy faith hath saved thee; go in peace,"
Christ said. He saw what you brought, your very self
to His feet, not pious words, our recipe.

Maybe you saunter into this church in heels
and short skirts. Maybe we see your breasts and frown
as if our curves are shameful to reveal.

I am tangled in your story, confounded
by the heat you bring to this place afraid of fire,
but for women to condemn our flesh? Unsound.

Christ understood the depth of your desire
present when He died. Later, He found you. "Mary,"
His voice like perfume. Your fire He admired.

Santa María, saint who loved much, accompany
me, who like the Pharisees am quick to judge.
Help me to release my fire, to feel its sanctity.

Saint Christopher |

San Cristóbal

Do you too miss the old days?
We're alone now, so I can return you
to your place and light a candle.
    Protect us, Saint Christopher.
Forgive me for hiding you, but
you're out of favor, an unofficial saint
not enough proof I hear.

Not enough proof. How can they say this
in a church. What happened to faith?
Thrown out like the Latin.
    Protégenos, San Cristóbal.
Hear that rain thrash the windows?
In such storms we need a giant like you
who understands the river's voices.

You understand the river's voices,
know we always pray for rain
since this dry land drinks in gulps.
    Protect us, Saint Christopher.
At your height, surely you understand
too much of even good things
can become burdens, ¿no?

He was no burden, the smiling Child
who climbed your body's twenty feet onto
your shoulder, a purposeful boy.
    Protégenos, San Cristóbal.
Like you'd carried others across
the swirling river, you set off again
as we set off daily from the shore of sleep.

You set off from the shore into
a whirlwind, clutched Him as we should
hold all children in life's stormy river.
                    Protect us, Saint Christopher.
But I fear the children can no longer
count on us who must seem like giants
peering down at their question-mark faces.

Your face was a question mark when
He grew heavier with each step
until you gasped, "Who are you?"
                    Protégenos, San Cristóbal.
He said you carried the weight of the world,
the Child, the mighty king you'd sought,
who smiled at your profound "Who are you?"

"Who are you?" The question echoes
through this church whose adobe may melt
if you don't silence the rain.
                    Protect us, Saint Christopher.
I've ordered each of my children
to keep your medal in their car. Yes, ordered.
My firmness comforts them.

You comfort me, here until the rain exhausts itself
as I will someday grow silent.
My quiet husband doubts my scoldings will ever cease.
                    Protégenos, San Cristóbal.
If I fall asleep, forgive me, Dear Friends.
Please walk here, chat among yourselves.
Help your Carmen across the treacherous river to faith.

Santa Ana

Rru-rru-que-rru-rru,
que tan, tan, tan,
Señora Santa Ana,
carita de luna,
Duerme esta niña
que tengo en la cuna.

Rock, rocking my babies,
rru-rru-que-rru-rru,
I sang your lullaby,
called you Santa Ana,
wrinkled little moon-face,
rru-rru-que-rru-rru,
my haloed abuela
who brought sleep in your hands
soft as a well-washed blanket,
tan, tan, tan.

Braiding water and your voice,
rru - rru,
you poured yourself into
your garden that first spring
with Joaquín, scented beds
rru-rru-que-rru-rru,
with your breath, nights opened
your arms and mouth praying
to swell like a budding moon,
que tan, tan, tan.

Watering seedlings full of hope,
rru-rru-que-rru-rru,
you hear others' babies.
You kneel, tend lilies that peek
from cold soil. Twenty years,
rru - rru,
you cover them with sighs
and unused diapers, sing
lullabies old in your mouth,
tan   tan.

Carita de luna,
rru - rru,
you sit alone and watch
a nervous mama bird,
beak to beak with its chick,
rru - rru.
Joaquín's back bends in silence,
and your voice trembles, but you sing
to the garden and yourself,
tan   tan.

Full of faith, you hear
rru - rru,
an angel whisper, "Run, kiss
Joaquín's wrinkled face."
Lip to lip, you feel within
rru-rru-que-rru-rru,
a wisp of music. You lift
your arms wide and spin
in grace, your mouth open.
Tan. Tan. Tan.

You and I hugged our daughters,
    rru-rru-que-rru-rru,
brought their bodies to books,
showed them how words enter,
grow inside us, bud, bloom,
    rru - rru.
Grandmother of grandmothers,
bless all women. Help us hear
grace, the music inside,
    tan, tan.

Saint Clare |
Santa Clara

Ve-ni Cre-a-tor Spi-ri-tus,

Let me rub your bare feet, Saint Clare,
like I rubbed Mamá's her last year.

Clara. Your mother knew, heard
in prayer you'd shine, a clear light.

Ve-ni Cre-a-tor Spi-ri-tus,

the hymn Francis and candles sang
the night you walked unscared into poverty.

At eighteen, I wanted a certain air,
red shoes, dresses to make boys stare, wink.

Ve-ni Cre-a-tor Spi-ri-tus,

Leaving comfort behind, you bowed
your head and Francis cut your long hair.

Without despair, you tied the rough
habit with a cord, knotted to Christ.

Ve-ni Cre-a-tor Spi-ri-tus,

You removed a pair of pretty shoes,
prepared for years of cold floors,

gathered women, even your mother,
to your spare life, the riches within.

Ve-ni Cre-a-tor Spi-ri-tus,

You shook your head to meat, shoes, beds,
entered the rare interior journey.

I'll sing, rub your bare feet, Saint Clare,
woman who knew the power of prayer.

Ve-ni Cre-a-tor Spi-ri-tus,

Armed men couldn't tear your sister
away, despaired at her immovable weight,

and the monstrance you raised at attacking
soldiers, stopped their bravery mid-air.

Ve-ni Cre-a-tor Spi-ri-tus,

But it's your bare feet worry me.
We're an odd pair, Saint Clare.

We both have a flair for needlework,
smile replacing threadbare altar linens,

Ve-ni Cre-a-tor Spi-ri-tus,

know the bare white cloth, a needle's eye,
the gentle pulling toward beauty,

retreat to our quiet gardens,
share delight at roses and prickly pear.

Ve-ni Cre-a-tor Spi-ri-tus,

We rise in the friend's laugh whose faith
in us dares us to exceed ourselves.

With what care you washed his feet. Francis.
Sister Death made your life more solitaire.

Ve-ni Cre-a-tor Spi-ri-tus,

You washed and kissed nuns' hard feet too,
declared humility with silent lips.

One Christmas, unable to rise, you heard
matins, stared. There: the manger on your wall.

Ve-ni Cre-a-tor Spi-ri-tus,

I rise early, light candles, but fear
my stubborn soul's still in disrepair.

Spark your Carmen's pale faith to flare.
Santa Clara, hear my prayer.

Saint Rose of Lima |
Santa Rosa de Lima

Your name blooms in our mouths, Rosita,
your stories too, the pink blossom
floating above your crib, your petaled
face, and at your death, your flesh perfume.

Why were you stubborn as a thorn?

We burrow into your legends sweet,
cringe at hints you peppered your cheeks,
dragged a cross around your parents' yard,
hacked your hair, punished your soft self.

In that yard, you built a hut, lived alone,
you, mosquitoes and spiders who'd pause
when you prayed, hoping to hear His words
again, "Rose of My Heart, be thou My spouse."

Why were you so stubborn?

You heard voices: Mary, her Child,
Saint Catherine. Did they speak en español,
a music vibrating in your bones
like cellos praising a sunset?

Over forty years I've strained to hear
one sound, a whispered YES or NO
from any of you, my holy family.
Your silence tests my faith, dear friends.

Why are you so stubborn?

Tell me, Rosita, what is holiness?
Is it the ecstasy of sacrifice,
the body chained, whipped, punctured, deprived
of even hard bread and the shelter of sleep?

I know you wished to suffer like Our Lord,
but we women bleed enough, Rosita.
The body isn't evil, just heavy,
flesh unaccustomed to flight.

Why were you stubborn as a thorn?

Let me bring you down to smell these roses
from my garden. I tell them about you.
Like children, they like a story. Please
soften me into a garden of light.

Our Lady of Sorrows |
Nuestra Señora de los Dolores

Seven swords pierced through your mother heart.
Simeon's prophecy prepared the way
for sorrow to leave its wrinkled mark.
Into Egypt you and Joseph fled dismayed
that human hands would itch to harm your son,
the dark-eyed boy who nervous gripped your hand.
The days you could not find Him you began
to walk with fear, feel its shadow, smell its dank
breath. What happened to the days of song and play,
you and your son like any other laughing pair?
How did you bear to see His body bathed
in blood, to see the flesh you fed, pierced?

Ave María, who are all sorrowful mothers,
open my ears to the wounded hearts who suffer.

Saint Raphael |

San Rafael

Saint Raphael, entrusted to foresee
danger, this day accompany our children
as they begin another journey.

They come, they go. We seldom see
the children now. Hover by them.
Guide to Tobias, be their company.

Books say you chant, "Holy, holy, holy,"
your endless praises guarding
us, your charges, on our life's journey.

How I wish, like you, I could foresee
the illness and danger lurking.
Protect my vulnerable family.

You took the young Tobias to see
the life-giving river, then scooping
a silvery fish, taught him healing artistry.

He learned to feel our fingers' ability,
rubbed his father's blind eyes, rubbing
gently until his father again could see.

Come to our clear river. Accompany me,
find me such a healing fish, then
bathe these cloudy eyes. Mi santo, hear my plea.

Daily I pray for my children's safety.
How I miss stroking their petal skin.
Guard them from dangers you foresee.

A mother's hands live hungry to protect
skin of our skin. Shield mis niños
with your wings. Be their holy company.

I worry. You know me. If I can't see,
drift more and more within,
who'll fret and pray about my children's safety?

Silly Carmen forgets what faith should be,
not about fretting but praising,
"Holy, holy, holy," in the Spirit's company.

My old tías said, "My eyes don't see
clearly now, but hija, I sense a power within."
My stubborn heart inherits that ability.

Saint Raphael, entrusted to foresee,
this day and every day, accompany our children
on their winding and uncertain journey.

Saint Michael the Archangel |
San Miguel Arcángel

From ese feo,
deliver us.

You who visit
that place of light
and perfect temperature
where there's never
a dust storm,
From all evil,
deliver us.

You who fly
back and forth
at no charge and never
feel your ankles swell
waiting in line,
From all evil,
deliver us.

You who arrive
shining with armor
and spear, ready to pierce
lurking evil
with the force of justice,
From all evil,
deliver us.

You who can pierce
those whose spiked words,
sting us with hate,
dip your spear into
their corroding poison and thrust.
From all evil,
deliver us.

Pierce landlords fat
with selfishness, rubbing
their hands through others' money.
Give them a good jab
for Carmen la sacristana,
    From all evil,
    deliver us.

Pierce men who strike
women and children,
ignore the terror in their eyes.
Sharpen your spear
and poke them with icy fear,
    From all evil,
    deliver us.

Pierce fancy thieves
whose oily words steal
our land, pride, dignity.
Wriggle your spear
in their flabby egos,
    From all evil,
    deliver us.

Pierce pious hypocrites
who gossip then come
wailing their rosaries.
Prick their mean tongues
until they repent.
    From all evil,
    deliver us.

I like your fire,
anger my old friend.
I too must charge,
ay, plunge my words –
into my own hard heart.
    From our evil,
    deliver us.

Saint Theresa of Lisieux |
    Santa Teresa de Lisieux

Rose bushes are miracles,
scented puzzles, aren't they, Teresita?
From all that thorny wood, a bud
appears, a sealed, green envelope.

You said your body was an envelope.
How we like to stare
at its familiar mold.
I saw your photo, but I like
your statue better. Eighty,
and I'm still attached to surfaces.

You lived briefly, as flowers do,
and when you died, a shower
of roses fell as you'd promised.
You became our image of a saint,
a young virgin, your body hidden,
your face smooth, a movie-star saint.

If you're pink honey, I'm
old vinegar today. Me and my moods.
There's a tiger loose inside me,
and the tiger has my face.
Books say you knew depression
so you know. Your humanity
comforts me more than
your unchanging expression.

I want a heaven full
of fighters, not just singers
and silent virgins,
or I won't feel at home.
The good women here,
grandmothers and old tías,
they'll heat the place.

I'm tired, headaches,
two houses to clean,
my husband's sighs
like cobwebs I sweep,
and my children need jobs.
I want to ask the help
of the real you,
to honor what you were
not what we've made you.

Help me to find my way,
again to pick up all that I am,
the thorniness of me.
With faith, may I return
to the rhythm of my work,
the green mystery within.

The Guardian Angels |

Los Angeles de la Guarda

Such days, I know you're here,
gold, feathered specks
that nudge, whisper,
"Warm them with your inner light."

Such days, the river and children laugh,
the sounds like tumbling bells
releasing their joy
unable to contain the secret
I once knew. Their lightness eludes
our height. We kneel,
closer again to earth
from which we can rise, transformed.

I'd pray to you back then, Angelito,
promise your Carmen would be very good if
you'd one day take my hand, stroll
the starry paths of heaven, past
diamond castles trimmed in gold and silver,
a shine to hurt the eyes,
but nothing hurts in heaven,
not our knees,
not our heads,
not our hearts.

Well, now it's too late
for promises, and I've seen heaven.
Aquí. In these hills,
the houses of glowing adobe
like rounded loaves,
light sliding but also rising,
the clear gold of wild grasses,
of swirling pollen,
of frog eyes humming,

birds sailing their songs,
old men whistling their dreams,
our children teasing,
a hundred candles at prayer,
the gold scent
nourishing and necessary,
like fresh bread, like this land
baking in the desert sun
that bakes me, and when I'm done,
I'll join the light.

Saint Francis of Assisi |

San Francisco de Asís

Brother Sun, a warm greeting.
Wind sings green. I bring armfuls
of flowers, joy, such colors rising
to grace this day of pet blessings.

To grace this day of pet blessings,
and honor you, Brother Francis,
who heard the music of the earth,
song gathered and sent fluttering.

Song gathered and sent fluttering
into laughter, shouts, children parading
their dogs, lizards, cats, birds, toads, mice,
a lively line of squirmings.

A lively line of squirmings.
Manito, remember the worm,
the boy extending his palm,
his poverty confirming?

His poverty confirming,
with Brother Worm teaching me praise,
to listen to goats, donkeys, quail,
even fish, life's song affirming.

Even fish, life's song affirming,
so why, with all this gray hair
do I frown at muddy children, pets?
Your Carmen pokey at learning.

Your Carmen pokey at learning,
and yet I know you kissed lepers,
pressed yourself into what you feared,
transformed by your holy yearning.

Transformed by your holy yearning,
rolling in snow, on thorns to still
your body, Brother Ass, while I
stuff myself, to old sins returning.

Stuff myself, to old sins returning
like talking when there's work to do.
Sweet and sour children will soon stream
to my stern nose upturning.

To my stern nose upturning
while you hear their interior
light, flickering hum of the life-wick
within our fragile skin, glowing.

Within our fragile skin, glowing,
Christ's wounds on your flesh streaming
light, but had you come, ragged here,
I fear you'd see Carmen frowning.

I fear you'd see Carmen frowning.
Would I have stopped those pelting you?
Why can't I risk myself?
My silly pride's unsound.

My silly pride's unsound
while you softened a wolf
your words like keys freeing him,
his gentleness unbound.

His gentleness unbound.
Ah. How you would place your worn hands
on all we bring – turtles, roosters, hens.
You'd pray, each life affirming.

You'd pray, each life affirming,
me? Deceived by surfaces while larks
knew your spark, sang their morning song,
the evening your heart ceased burning.

The evening your heart ceased burning
yet those last years unable to see
but seeing the flame even
within Sister Pebble, blazing.

Within Sister Pebble, blazing
your eyes danced with each candle flame
you'd not bruise with your breath.
Teach me such attentive gazing.

Teach me such attentive gazing
before the squirming children come,
I raise my arms to Brother Sun
and pray to learn the joy of praising.

Saint Teresa of Avila |
Santa Teresa de Ávila

"If I had not been so wicked . . ."
Your words reveal your character,
Stern, aware of hell's punishments,
Forever, ever and ever.

A child, you raced hand in hand
with your brother, shortcut to heaven,
a beheading by Moors, savored
the honey taste of martyrdom,
your soul zipping to joy. Wicked?
No. Though stern, I hear your humor,
"I can be had for a sardine,"
life like "a night in a bad inn."
Sly, forever peering inside,
"If I had not been so wicked . . ."

Restless. What to do with so much you?
Come walk around this church, compose
letters, books. Your charms will make
priests dizzy, woman at forty who
finds herself again, as we do
if blessed. Take me to His Majesty's
whispers, white light enters, lifts
us from this wood. You urge yourself,
"Cold simpleton, not think much, love much."
Your words reveal your character.

Years you vomited. Was it passion
you spewed, an excess of spirit,
your body, like a rigid rose,
unable to hold such longings?
The mind can't save us forever.
Even one ever blinding as yours
burrowed to lose consciousness
from pain of self-entanglement,
in terror sought blessed safety,
stern, aware of hell's punishments.

Head aching, you demanded prayer,
poverty, purity, but savored
"holy madness," cleaned out cozy
convents like you purged your body,
yet opened your lips to His, sweet face
transporting you. Your body,
no pastel lover, knew fire, burned
gloriously. Kindle my spirit,
Doctora, set me burning to light
forever, ever and ever.

The Good Shepherdess |
La Buena Pastora

Santa María, Madre Mía, your sparrows tugged
    me from dreams, insistent beauty.
            The ignorant call this birdsong ordinary.
No voice lifted in praise is ordinary
    but joyful mystery like these roses. And my children.

Who could sleep on such a day? In the garden, I feared
    I'd drift high into the sea of light.
          To catch myself, I bent into these blooms,
into my plants shining in the morning breeze
    like green candles, the garden an altar of praise.

Santa María, Buena Pastora, I bring what earth releases
    from itself as we can from our roots and thorns
          release light, interior grace, the joyful mystery
of rhythms and transformation, this gold land
    humming with butterflies, buds, our spirits.

I hear your wise melody, "Come, vengan,"
    you sing, ignore our human bickering,
         gather us, your arms wide as the desert,
evening soft, shelter from rumors
    of flames, chains, diablitos crooning our names.

"Come, vengan," you sing, feed us perfume,
    such extravangance to offer us roses, our mouths
        scented, full of pink we chew, nuzzle
closer to your skirt's sweet green-grass smell,
    to our mother's lavish love holding us with petals, song.

Madre Mía, teach your cranky Carmen the practicality
of beauty, its joyful mystery necessary as bread.
The saints shine in grace, warm
these creaky bones with their light.
Like your sparrows, I raise my voice in praise.

Notes on the Saints ❧ and Their Feast Days

Notes on the Saints and Their Feast Days |

Prayer to the Saints / Oración a los Santos.
The feast of All Saints, also known as All Hallows' Day, precedes All Souls' Day, when the faithful departed are remembered with the words, "Eternal rest grant unto them, O Lord, and let perpetual light shine upon them." This poem is based on a Spanish rhyming litany imploring help in finding a husband. All Saints' Day is celebrated on November 1.

Saint Martin of Porres / San Martín de Porres,
the illegitimate son of a Spaniard and a Panamanian woman, was born in Lima, Peru, in 1579 and died in 1639. Apprenticed as a barber-surgeon, when young he became a Dominican lay brother who cared for orphans, for the sick, and particularly for black slaves. The feast day of this patron saint of social justice is November 3.

Saint Gertrude the Great / Santa Gertrudis la Magna,
an early feminist who lived approximately from 1256 to 1301, is an author known for her devotion to the Sacred Heart. A German medievel mystic, she began living at the Benedictine monastery at Helfta in her childhood. Her writings, which include *The Herald of God's Loving-Kindness,* are often about her visions. Her works were republished in the sixteenth century and became popular in Spain. She thus became a model for Saint Teresa of Ávila. Patron saint of the West Indies and of students, her feast day is November 16.

Saint Barbara / Santa Bárbara
is the legendary daughter of the jealous King Dioscorus. To prevent possible suitors from seeing his beautiful daughter, the king locked her in a tower. Enraged when he learned that Barbara had become a Christian, he beheaded her and was struck by lightning. She is

invoked as protection against thunderstorms and lightning and is the patron saint of architects and builders. The feast day of this fourth-century martyr is December 4.

Our Lady of Guadalupe / Nuestra Señora de Guadalupe
is the patron saint of the Americas who appeared in Mexico to Juan Diego on the hill of Tepeyac, requesting that a shrine be built there in her honor. As a sign to the bishop, Our Lady caused roses to bloom on the dry landscape and her image to appear on Juan Diego's tunic which is on display at her basilica in Mexico City. Her feast day is December 12.

The Nativity / El Nacimiento,
preceded by the season of Advent, four weeks of preparing spiritually for the birth of Christ, is celebrated December 25.

The Holy Child of Atocha / El Santo Niño de Atocha
is the Christ Child in pilgrim garb. Usually seated, He holds both a basket and a staff topped with a small water gourd. The statue of Nuestra Señora in Atocha, Spain, holds her Son, who was said to enter Moorish prisons at night to give bread and water to incarcerated Spaniards. Devotion to this Child is popular in Mexico and the Southwest, a Boy who wears out His tiny shoes as He aids those in mines and prisons. The feast day of El Santo Niño, whose aid is sought for travelers and the incarcerated, is December 25.

The Holy Family / La Sagrada Familia
is the holy trio of the Child Jesus, Mary, and Joseph. The feast of the Holy Family is celebrated the first or third Sunday after January 6.

Saint Joseph / San José,
a descendant of the royal house of David, is said to have been a poor carpenter in Nazareth. Mary's husband and foster father to Jesus, he was an extremely virtuous man. The patron saint of fathers, the universal church, and a happy death, his feast day is March 19.

Our Lady of the Annunciation / Nuestra Señora de la Anunciación.
Celebrated nine months before Christmas, this feast, which reminds
us of the appearance of the angel Gabriel in Galilee, or Nazareth, to
announce to Mary that she would give birth to a son and that her
older cousin Elizabeth had also conceived, is celebrated on March 25.

The Stations of the Cross / La Vía Crucis
are reminders of Christ's suffering and provide an opportunity for
Catholics to accompany Christ on His sad and painful journey from
His condemnation to death to His being placed in the sepulchre.
Many Catholic churches have the fourteen events depicted on
church walls. The faithful walk from Station to Station praying
alone or participate in a formal service which can include prayers,
singing, and meditation.

Death / La Muerte,
also known as Doña Sebastiana, is depicted as a skeletal woman, not
a saint but a stark reminder of the horror of a "bad" death.

Christ on the Cross / Nuestro Señor Crucificado
is an image sad and compelling to Christians and non-Christians, a
reminder of our capacity to hurt one another, physically as well as
psychologically. Special veneration is paid to this image on Good
Friday.

Saint Isidore / San Ysidro
was a devout farm laborer who worked outside of Madrid in the
twelfth century. Some sources say he worked for Juan de Vargas, an
ancestor of Diego de Vargas who reconquered New Mexico in 1692
after the Pueblo Revolt. The feast day of the patron saint of farmers,
often petitioned for rain, is May 15.

The Holy Spirit / El Espíritu Santo,
also known as the Holy Ghost, is the third person of the Trinity,
often depicted as a tongue of fire or a dove, a symbol of

enlightenment. The feast of the descent of the Holy Spirit is celebrated on Pentecost, originally the fiftieth day after Passover, now the seventh Sunday after Easter.

Saint Pascal Baylon / San Pascual Bailón,
born in Torre Hermosa, Spain, near Aragón, lived from 1540 to 1592. A shepherd as a boy, he became a lay brother of the barefoot Franciscans and had an intense devotion to the Eucharist. The patron of shepherds, he is also popular in Mexico and New Mexico as a patron saint of cooks. His feast day is May 17.

Saint Rita / Santa Rita
was born in Cascia, Italy, in 1381 and died in 1457. Though she wished to be a nun, she endured an unhappy and abusive arranged marriage until her husband was murdered. She prayed that her two sons would not avenge their father's death, and Saint Rita was supposedly relieved when her sons died of an illness. She eventually joined an Augustinian convent where a thorn from Christ's crown pierced her forehead during one of her mystical experiences. Like Saint Jude, she is a patron saint of impossible cases. The feast day of la abogada de los casos imposibles is May 22.

The Visitation / La Visitación
commemorates Mary's visit to her older cousin Elizabeth. When the angel Gabriel announced to Mary that she would give birth, he also told Mary that her cousin, wife of Zacharias, was also expecting. The couple had long given up hope of having a child. Their son, Jesus' cousin, was John the Baptist. The Visitation, the second of the joyful mysteries of the rosary, and the Queenship of Mary are celebrated on May 31.

Saint Anthony of Padua / San Antonio de Padua
lived from 1195 to 1231. Born in Lisbon as Fernando Martín de Bulholm, he became a Franciscan and preached all over Italy

establishing a reputation as an ardent orator. Patron saint of the poor and of lost articles, the feast day of this Doctor of the Church is June 13.

Saint Liberata / Santa Librada,
a legendary European saint, is said to have been a virgin martyr crucified in the third century. She is also venerated as Livrade in France, Uncumber in England, and Kümmernis / Wilgefortis, meaning "strong virgin," in Germany. Her name comes from her purported prayer on the cross that those who pray to her will be freed from their burdens, unencumbered. In England, unhappy brides are said to leave this saint a sack of oats so that the horses of unwelcome husbands will carry them to the devil. Though some believe her image is actually a clothed crucifix mistaken in the past for a bearded woman, this unofficial saint is viewed by others as the patron of abused women. Her feast day was July 20.

Saint Mary Magdalen / Santa María Magdalena
is depicted as the sinful woman who washed Christ's feet with her tears and dried them with her hair. She is with Him at the Crucifixion and is the first to see Him after the Resurrection. In an interesting juxtaposition, this saint is prayed to both by repentant sinners and by those interested in the contemplative life. Her feast day is July 22.

Saint Christopher / San Cristóbal
was a giant who carried travelers across a river. The name Christopher in Greek means Christ bearer, appropriate since this giant was said to have carried the Christ Child on his shoulders. The patron saint of motorists, Chistopher is no longer in the Roman Catholic liturgical calendar. His feast day was July 24.

Saint Anne / Santa Ana,
Mary's mother and Jesus' grandmother, was married to Joachim.

Though little is known about her, tradition says that she was childless for years, yet gave birth to Mary at forty. The patron saint of pregnant women, mothers, and grandmothers, her feast day is July 26.

Saint Clare / Santa Clara,
a native of Assisi, lived approximately from 1193 to 1253. She adopted the rule of Saint Francis and founded the Poor Ladies, now known as the Poor Clares, a strict religious order. The patron saint of embroiderers, those with sore eyes, and television, her feast day is August 11.

Saint Rose of Lima / Santa Rosa de Lima,
whose name was actually Isabel de Santa María de Flores, lived from 1586 to 1617 and is often referred to as the first New World saint. She joined the Third Order of Saint Dominic and spent most of her life as a recluse in her parents' garden. The feast day of this patron saint of florists and of South America is August 23.

Our Sorrowful Mother / La Dolorosa
is the manifestation of Mary and her sorrows at the time of her Son's suffering. Her griefs are often depicted as swords piercing her heart. The feast of the Seven Sorrows of the Blessed Virgin Mary is September 15.

Saint Raphael the Archangel / San Rafael el Arcángel,
whose name means "God has healed," appears in the Book of Tobit. The feast day of the patron of travelers and those with eye trouble was October 24 but is now celebrated as part of the feast of the three archangels on September 29.

Saint Michael the Archangel / San Miguel Arcángel,
the patron of law enforcement officers and protector of the church, leads the celestial forces in their struggle against evil. The feast of

the archangels Michael, Gabriel, and Raphael, the second of the nine choirs of angels, is celebrated September 29.

Saint Theresa of Lisieux / Santa Teresa de Lisieux,
the popular saint known as "Little Flower of Jesus," lived from 1873 to 1897. Born in Alençon, Normandy, one of nine children, she was named Marie Françoise Martin. Her mother died when she was five, which may in part explain her deep devotion to Mary as Mother. Determined to become a nun, at fifteen she finally received special permission to join the Carmelite order to which her sisters belonged, taking the name Theresa of the Child Jesus and the Holy Face. The prioress, her sister, in time instructed Theresa to write about her childhood and life. The result was Saint Theresa's spiritual autobiography, *The Story of a Soul,* which includes her description of what she called "her little way" of enduring life's annoyances. When it was published after her death from tuberculosis at a young age, the book quickly achieved a following and brought attention to the previously unknown Carmelite. The patron saint of florists and foreign missions, her feast day is October 1.

The Guardian Angels / Los Angeles de la Guarda,
messengers from God, are our physical and spiritual protectors on earth. Their feast day is October 2.

Saint Francis of Assisi / San Francisco de Asís,
born Giovanni Bernardone, lived from 1181 to 1226. He renounced his family's wealth and dreams of knighthood to found the Franciscan Orders, committing himself to "Lady Poverty." The feast day of this patron saint of animals, Italy, and ecology is October 4.

Saint Teresa of Avila / Santa Teresa de Ávila,
also known as the Great Saint Teresa, Teresa de Cepeda y Ahumada, was born in 1515 in Ávila, Spain, and died in 1582. A mystic, author of *Autobiography, The Way of Perfection,* and *The Interior Castle,*

she reformed the Carmelite Order and wrote extensively. In 1970, she was named the first woman Doctor of the Church, a title given to ecclesiastical writers whose work is of significance to Church doctrine. A writer with a playful sense of humor, she said, "God deliver me from sullen saints." The feast day of the patron saint of those suffering from headaches is October 15.

The Good Shepherdess / La Buena Pastora
is a relatively unknown manifestation of Mary and has no feast day observance. Mary is depicted in a pastoral setting surrounded by sheep.

Credits |

[Page 12] Prayer to the Saints, altar screen by Rafael Aragón. Photographer: Blair Clark. International Folk Art Foundation Collections at the Museum of International Folk Art, Museum of New Mexico, Santa Fe, New Mexico.

[Page 15] Saint Martin of Porres / Ayacucho, Ayacucho, Peru. Photographer: Michel Monteaux. From the Girard Foundation Collection at the Museum of International Folk Art, Museum of New Mexico.

[Page 18] Saint Gertrude, altar screen by Rafael Aragón. Photographer: Blair Clark. International Folk Art Foundation Collections at the Museum of International Folk Art.

[Page 21] Saint Barbara, by the Truchas Master. Photographer: unknown. Cady Wells Bequest to the Museum of New Mexico, Museum of International Folk Art.

[Page 23] Our Lady of Guadalupe, by Rafael Aragón. Photographer: Blair Clark. Cady Wells Bequest to the Museum of New Mexico, Museum of International Folk Art.

[Page 25] The Nativity / El Nacimiento by José Mondragón. Photographer: Blair Clark. Gift of the Historical Society of New Mexico to the Museum of New Mexico, Museum of International Folk Art.

[Page 26] Holy Child of Atocha / Santo Niño, by Victoria López, 1980 (L.I.1993-087-01). Photographer: Blair Clark. Archdiocese of Santa Fe Collection in the Museum of New Mexico, Museum of International Folk Art.

[Page 30] The Holy Family, by Charlie Carrillo. Photographer: Blair Clark. Museum of New Mexico Collections, Museum of International Folk Art.

[Page 33] Saint Joseph / San José by Laguna Santero. Photographer: Blair Clark. Spanish Colonial Arts Society, Inc. Collection on loan to the Museum of New Mexico, Museum of International Folk Art.

[Page 34] Our Lady of the Annunciation (El Alma de María). Photographer: Blair Clark. Spanish Colonial Arts Society, Inc. Collection on loan to the Museum of New Mexico, Museum of International Folk Art.

[Page 39] Stations of the Cross, Nuestro Padre Jesús Nazareno, by Molleno (L.5.75–31). Photographer: Blair Clark. Spanish Colonial Arts Society, Inc. Collection on loan to the Museum of New Mexico, Museum of International Folk Art.

[Page 41] Death / La Muerte, García, Colorado. Photographer: Blair Clark. Spanish Colonial Arts Society, Inc. Collection on loan to the Museum of New Mexico, Museum of International Folk Art.

[Page 44] Crucifijo / Crucifix, New Mexico, ca. 1840. Photographer: Art Taylor. Spanish Colonial Arts Society, Inc. Collection on loan to the Museum of New Mexico, Museum of International Folk Art.

[Page 47] Saint Isidore / San Isidro / San Ysidro Labrador by José Benito Orteg. Photographer: Blair Clark. Cady Wells Bequest to the Museum of New Mexico, Museum of International Folk Art.

[Page 48] Holy Spirit. Photographer: unknown. Cady Wells Bequest to the Museum of New Mexico, Museum of International Folk Art.

[Page 53] Saint Pascal, (A.77.44–1) colcha embroidery by Frances Graves. Photographer: unknown. Museum of New Mexico Collections, Museum of International Folk Art.

[Page 55] Saint Rita, the Quill Pen Santero. Photographer: unknown. Museum of New Mexico Collections, Museum of International Folk Art.

[Page 59] Visitation, La Visita. Photographer: Blair Clark. Museum of New Mexico Collections, Museum of International Folk Art.

[Page 60] Saint Anthony of Padua by Zoraida and Eulogio Ortega. Photographer: Blair Clark. Spanish Colonial Arts Society, Inc. Collection on loan to the Museum of New Mexico, Museum of International Folk Art.

[Page 65] Saint Liberata. Photographer: Michel Monteaux. From the Girard Foundation Collection at the Museum of International Folk Art, Museum of New Mexico.

[Page 67] Mary Magdalene / Santa María Magdalena by José Aragón, San Cristóbal, New Mexico. Photographer: Blair Clark. International Folk Art Collections at the Museum of International Folk Art.

[Page 71] Saint Christopher, by Raphael Aragón. Photographer: unknown. Spanish Colonial Arts Society, Inc. Collection on loan to the Museum of New Mexico, Museum of International Folk Art.

[Page 73] Saint Anne / Santa Ana by Ellen Chavez de Leitner. Photographer: Blair Clark. International Folk Art Collections at the Museum of International Folk Art.

[Page 76] Saint Clare of Assisi by Clairvaux McFarland, OSF. Photograph furnished by the artist.

[Page 80 *detail*, 82] Saint Rose of Lima by David Gonzales (FA 91.33–1). Photographer: Blair Clark. International Folk Art Collections at the Museum of International Folk Art.

[Page 84] Our Lady of Sorrows. Photographer: Blair Clark. Gift of the Historical Society of New Mexico to the Museum of New Mexico, Museum of International Folk Art.

[Page 86] Saint Raphael / San Rafael, by Donna Wright de Romero, 1992 (FA 1992.82–2). Photographer: Blair Clark. International Folk Art Collections at the Museum of International Folk Art.

[Page 90] Saint Michael / San Miguel, by Luis Tapia. Photographer: Blair Clark. Spanish Colonial Arts Society, Inc. Collection on loan to the Museum of New Mexico, Museum of International Folk Art.

[Page 97] Guardian Angel by José Aragón, New Mexico. Photographer: Blair Clark. Cady Wells bequest to the Museum of New Mexico, Museum of International Folk Art.

[Page 98] Saint Francis of Assisi / San Francisco de Asís by Luis Aragón (A.68.27–1). Photographer: Art Taylor. Museum of New Mexico Collections, Museum of International Folk Art.

[Page 102] St. Teresa of Ávila, by Rafael Aragón. Photographer: Blair Clark. Cady Wells bequest to the Museum of New Mexico, Museum of International Folk Art.

[Page 107] The Good Shepherdess. Photographer: Blair Clark. From the Girard Foundation Collection at the Museum of International Folk Art, Museum of New Mexico.

[Page 119] The Nativity/El Nacimiento. New Mexico, late eighteenth century. Photographer: Blair Clark. Gift of the Historical Society of New Mexico, Museum of International Folk Art.

Acknowledgments |

Many thanks to the Museum of International Folk Art in Santa Fe, New Mexico, tierra sagrada, for the quick willingness to allow us to enrich this book with images from the Museum's collections. I am particularly grateful for the enthusiasm and assistance of Eleanore Voutselas. I also appreciate the help of Judith Sellars, Robin Farwell Gavin, and Mariah Sacoman at the Museum, Jane Gillentine at the School of American Research, and John Drury for his attentive reading of the manuscript and helpful suggestions.

The power of others' faith in us never ceases to amaze me. I'm deeply grateful for the unswerving faith of my family, particularly Aunt Chole who daily prays for me; my mother, Estela Mora; my husband, Vern Scarborough, who read every raw poem; my siblings, Cissy, Stella, and Anthony; and my children, Bill, Libby, and Cissy. All endure my moans.